Getting
NOTICED
by Your
Perfect Man
Bitter and Beauty

Based on

THE BOOK OF RUTH

Ruth and Naomi

Written by

By Ernest L. Sanders
A Bishop in the Episcopal Church of Jesus

PREFACE

The book is dedicated to some very special ladies, my maternal mother Mrs. Annie Sanders and my church mothers.   Mrs. Georgia Lee Waites, Nettie Robins and Auntie Ruth Taylor who have made all the difference in my life. If I achieve anything at all in life, it is to their credit and a result of my receiving the blessings of Almighty God. This Book is also dedicated to my sisters Brenda, Queenie, Mary and Vanessa. These are exciting, special and wonderful women in my life. To my granddaughters Myia, Abbi, Kylee, and a special God-daughter Tamyra James

Life affords us many opportunities to meet people who are instrumental to our success by showing exceptional love and concern for our well-being. God has granted me the special gift of many such people in my life especially Mrs. Nettie M. Nobles Robbins, a mother, a friend, and mentors.

Special dedication to Dr. Carrie M. Jones

Tables of Contents

Introduction

M.O.V.E.
No Violence
Show Yourself

Chapter One

Chapter Two

Chapter Three

Chapter Four

The Conclusion of the Matter

Introduction

There are no good men!
All the good men are married, dead or in jail!
I just cannot find a man to marry or live with!!!
I am not compatible with anyone!!!
I am not compatible with anyone else!!!
I'll just be by myself!!!
I can do bad all by myself!!!

These are statements heard every day and uttered by women of all race creed and color. The author of this book disagrees with these statements. God would certainly be an unjust God to have created such a situation without a solution. There are available men of all races ready for a personal and committed relationship of all kind. The question is not whether or not there are men, but are there women prepared to receive these men into their lives. God has promised to give us the desires of our hearts. God created woman for man and man for woman. Since God is the centerpiece in this relationship, we should certainly consider what He has to say? The scripture gives directions on how to form and maintain a good and prosperous relationship. There are detailed accountings of what is a godly man and woman. It gives details on what should be expected of the relationship as well as the order of the relationship and how the relationship is formed and blessed.

Unfortunately, the idea of a good man in the eyes of most women is one that has a good job, money, education and a good physically appearance. Certainly, some of these qualities are necessary and all should be considered. However, along with these are many other qualities that should be considered. Are they good sex partners? Conversationalist? Ready for action in crunch time? Adventurous? There are many others included, but are not limited to things like a good heart, a kind spirit, proper manners, respectable, good morals and a relationship with God. Can he be led or is he a leader? Can I or will I follow his lead? Relationship is complicated and becomes more complicated if we invest time and energy into the wrong person. Computer dating has become a part of our society and it certainly has a place. Unfortunately, the computer can only respond to what is entered into the hard drive We are not always truthful with the computer and the computer cannot read the real person. We live in a world where there are limited value systems. Economics, social status and who's who have replaced true family values. What is the economics of a good father or spouse? There is a saying today that there can be no romance without finance. How much finance is necessary and what does it qualify one for except acquiring of material things. Shouldn't we look further when determining who will be our life partner?

I believe that with the right romance, attitude and work, finance will come and social status will be gained. No one is teaching the basic principles of love and respect for a relationship. Intimacy is a necessary part of relationship, both in bed and out. Loyalty and responsibility are vital feeling as well as sexual organisms. If a man loves God and the things of God, it is not a guarantee of a perfect relationship, but it is a good start. There are no absolutes that a man or woman in the church will make a perfect mate, but it certainly gives you a head start.

This author does not by any means say that a man should not be employed even if he is wealthy. Most accumulation of wealth requires some form of physical and mental motivation. A man that will not work will not do much else. He must have a dream, a desire or a vision for himself and the relationship. She must agree with the dream. The two cannot walk together unless there is an agreement. It is not always necessary that she is actively involved in the day to day operation of the dream, but there must be emotional, spiritual and moral support.

M.O.V.E.

Mentor- Obedience-Visualization -Explanation

Faith is the ability to believe in oneself. Success in life is not a set of abstract circumstances but definite in how you think of yourself. It starts with a positive attitude toward your own bruises, scars and imperfections. Faith starts with and ends with YOU and God. Faith in oneself is personal. YOU must believe in yourself and what God has done and is doing with you. YOU didn't make you, GOD DID and He knew exactly what He was doing. Now, you can complain, grumble and grieve all you want, YOU are all YOU got. Putting on make-up, false hair, eyelashes and a tight fitting belt to hide what God has gifted you with is not going to always work. These items only seek to enhance the beauty that God has created. The real you will all show up one day despite false fittings. In the beginning of a relationship, let him/her know who you are from the crown of your head to your big toe nail. If the person cannot handle what is real so be it. A lie is temporary and to show anything but the real you are a lie. Maybe God did not make you for him. YOU cannot make anything happen but you can be 100% real. Being real is not for the other person, but for you. It is important for your self-esteem and emotional well-being that you be real. That is not to say, do not take good care of yourself, but be happy with you and not try to be happy because of who you think you need to be. Fat and fabulous is just as good as thin and grinning.   It is all in the attitude. Positive and productive attitudes lead to permanent and continual growth. Learn to grow physical, spiritually, economically, socially and into a positive state of self - awareness. It is all about faith in yourself and the belief that you are wonderful. Relationship is about developing confidence in self; learning about yourself and self - appreciation. Spend some me time with self, love self and respect what God has done with you.

LEARN to MOVE. There is nowhere in the Bible that anything happened because the person sat still or said nothing. You need to get-up. speak-up, dress up and show up. God gave you so give God something back to work with. God knows what you got and he knows what you need, and he knows who needs you. **LET'S MOVE**. It is hard to hit a MOVING target, but the chase is so much excitement. Put yourself out there and market the product. Take a walk, get involved in social activities, and be seen. Get in their eyesight. Home is a place to rest from all the activities you are involved in to make your life worthwhile. In the Book of Ruth, she was active, involved and exposed to the challenges presented by Boaz. Move into his eyesight. Don't chase or look desperate but keep him focused on you. The acronym MOVE means just that. Do not become stagnate, stale, dry and out of touch. The world is changing daily and you should change with it. Take the challenge to live life to its fullest. There is plenty of time to rest when you die. Life should be an adventure of joys, pains, failures, successes and relationships. Depression, checkout, slowdowns and timeouts are not options. Dreaming big, meeting challenges, conquering circumstances and overcoming obstacles is the order of the day. Move into your destiny that you have determined for your life. Obey the instincts of your heart and learn to survive any brokenness. Victory is assured because you breathe it, embrace it, and walk in it. Ecstasy is accepted as empowering, invigorating and refreshing. Fussing, frustrations, nagging and complaining is counter-productive to a happy relationship. Maximize every moment of life, minimize confusion and trim away every dead attitude that try to steal life. Move ! Move! and drink in the sweet nectar of life, show the beauty of you inside and out and trust God for success. You are no good to anyone else until you are good to yourself. Open yourself to love, joy and relationship. Bleed if you must, endure pain if it comes, but do not quit, compromise or checkout. Every day is your day..

Mentor

Mentor are to be guides, teachers, examples and sometimes our earthly heroes. Every relationship must have a mentor or an example to follow. God has provided many examples for us. Many time they exist in our own parents. Most parents and elderly couples in the church would consider it an honor to provide instructions and advice to couples, but most couples do not ask. The scripture requires the widow and elderly women of the church to instruct the younger women in how to raise their families and behave as women. It is also necessary for the woman seeking a mate for herself and a father for her children to at least know what the scripture says of a good husband and father. Couples should know their mate's history. Avoiding introducing you to their family or people with whom they are close may indicate shame, uncertainty, carefulness, carelessness, fear and sometimes downright dis-respect. A mentor will help you decide which of these things are important and provide guidance to improve or vacate the situation. A mentor helps you see straight, tells you the truth and loves you in your joys and pains. The mentor may or may not be emotionally involved and should always be truthful.

The relationship must have intimacy. Intimacy includes but is more than sexual closeness. This is an area that Christian do not like to discuss, but intimacy is not an option in a relationship. Ignoring intimacy is destructive to the growth of the relationship It must be passionate, wild and without restraints. Intimacy look deep inside of a person and brings out the real inner-self without reservations. Intimacy includes dreams, aspirations, desires and levels of consciousness. If you can touch that area of pleasure and bring the ultimate climax coupled with the love of God, the relationship will work.

Intimacy involves talking, sharing, laughing, and showing kindness to each other. The feeling is, "nothing is impossible to achieve together." Although marriage is the ultimate oneness, there is a oneness in relationships that must be achieve before marriage.

Mentoring is imitation of those who are successful. There is absolutely nothing wrong with finding a couple that you would like to imitate or grow into being and setting your standards according to what you observe. Psalm 37:37 states, "mark the perfect man and behold the upright; for the end of that man is peace". An age old principle in business and social arena is "if you want to be successful, attach yourself to successful people". If you want to be married attach yourself to those who have a successful, marriage. Remember relationships are not without problems but look for someone has who works through their problem and not become victims of the problems. If your friend, relative, or church member is divorced it is not impossible but highly unlikely they can give you good advice. Divorce oftentimes leaves pain, fears, prejudices, scars and opened wounds. Sometimes divorce is a release from pain. The residual affect can last a lifetime. Separation is often the result of temporary release from pain that oftentimes lead to divorce.

It is like half time in a football game. Rest a moment, take a breather and go back at it. The issue is not who was at fault but the marriage was unsuccessful. Fault is subject to who is telling the story. Negative people often, not always, breed negative people. Remember just because the marriage failed does not mean the people are failures. There are many valid reasons for separation and divorce. You must keep in mind that it is too much trouble to listen to the why of a failed relationship. It just takes too much energy to process other people problems. Find a positive, upbeat, successful, married person as your mentor. Less mess less stress. Be at your best physically, emotionally, and mentally when your new husband arrives. If you do not stockpile the junk, they will not have to move it to find you. You can become junk and only attract the junkman. It is vital to your success that you choose a successful mentor. One who has your best interest at heart. Friends and associates are not always good mentor.

Obedience

The second principle is to obey your mentor. No! your mentor does not have a set of instructions or a rule book on how to.... The mentor has lived a lifestyle and a way of well-being that has led to success with relationships. The mentor has been where you are headed and although it is a different time and different people the rules of engagement are the same. Good moral and ethical principles do not change. Obedience is seen as a dirty word in establishing and maintaining relationships. There is no desire to make you a "dummy", "yes person", or someone with no will. Obedience is submission to the authority of those who have a superior knowledge and experience. (Deuteronomy 11:26-28) Obedience is human behavior at its highest level. It is positioning oneself for a blessing. Trusting in the authority of someone else. Obedience is absolutely wonderful when exercised properly. People often hear and act according to what they hear without thought expecting a blessing. Obedience is hearing, trusting, submitting and surrendering yourself to life with pleasure.

   There will be many voices and great advisors but stay true to the mentor. There will voices critical, questioning and sometimes demeaning to the mentor. Stay focus! Ruth did as she was instructed by Naomi. You do not lose your so called independence by following instructions. If fact you cannot do anything without instruction and sometime we fail with the best instructions.

Obedience is more than saying "yes ma'am and yes sir. It is heart- felt, respect and a feeling of well-being. Obedience is not creating controversy but overcoming it, facing it and dispelling it.

Visualization

Visualization is the higher form of making things happen. Say to yourself, it is all about me because I can see me" Look into the mirror of life and see yourself. The same mirror shows our defects and shortcomings so look again and again if necessary until you get it right. If you cannot see your success, it will never happen. Seeing is believing and believing is success. Admit what is bothering you, what you do not like about you and change it if you must. Take time to evaluate you personally without input from anyone.

Visualize yourself as being in a relationship or married to your king. Without a vision you will perish. Think about what you want, need, and are willing to submit to. THAT'S RIGHT! SUMMIT TO? Even the weakest man wants to feel like a king and exercise some form of kingship and dominance. The strongest woman still need to be loved, held, kissed, desired and needed. Visualize the courtship, the tender embraces, hand holding, first kiss, the weakness of your body to touch, the loss of control at the sight, touch and hearing of your king voice. Visualize yourself as the queen of his life. Open your ears to the baritone voice of excellence, the strong firm arm of protection and the gently but firm hand of correction and care. It is about what you see.

Explanation

People spend so much time trying to explain themselves as to "why this" and "why that" and "how come" and "if only". forget it. Stop helping the enemy by pointing out your faults, shortcoming and errors. Stop making excuses for who you are not and explain with confidence who you are. Explain yourself and do not be shy about what you want and what is acceptable to you. Admit your fears, fantasies and positive points. Leave nothing to chance, explain yourself thoroughly. You do not need a bucket list or a list of what happened in the past. It is not important to your future. Openness is the key to a successful relationship. Silent moments should be used for reflections only. Talk about the subject you know the most about-YOU.

Leave your bucket list at home. That include what has happened to you in the past. It is not important nor good conversation. People listen to be nice but nobody want to know your past. They want to know your future.

NO Violence

DO NOT TOLERATE, ACCEPT, ENDURE, VIOLENCE OF ANY KIND, AT ANYTIME AND FROM ANYONE!!

Always remember that violence is not a part of the lifestyle you choose. Do not subject yourself to any kind of violence be it emotional, physical, mental or social. Apology after an experience of violence is unacccptable. There are no words that can make you feel good about violence. Violence is an automatic termination of all relationships. You cannot accept phone calls! There is an immediate blocking of the number and you should tell at least two other people of the incident. If the person persists in calling, writing or coming into your presence call the police and get a restraining order. This is serious business. There are no second chances or three strike you are out. One strike can affect your entire life so stop it now. Anger management, counseling, rehabilitation of a violent person is not acceptable when forming a relationship.

These are tools use to mask the violent behavior. GET OUT OF THE RELATIONSHIP!!! Whenever there are spoke, written words, body hits, implied or actual acts of violence stop immediately and run for your life. Make up may hide the bruises of violence but there is no medicine that can correct the mental pain of violence. When did you last see a queen with a black eye or bruised body and fragile mental state? If a woman is man's glory, what would make him deface, shame or bruise his glory? Submission should be because you are in love and not in fear. Hands were made for caressing and not hitting. Lips for kissing and not verbal abuse and feet for carrying her and not kicking. There are so many people who feels relationship can change a violent person. It cannot change but can control for a period of time. Unfortunately, this is time that you do not have. It is a job for which you do not make application.

Show Yourself

You got it! Flaunt it whatever it is. This is what you bring to the relationship-be it brain or body; prestige or power, you got it God gave it be proud of it. Never accept second class, either be first or not at all. No exceptions!!!!

First of all, you cannot get captured, married or anything else hidden in a corner. Stop hiding in church and sticking at home. Remember that he will look but not hard. Men are led by their mind and not brain. Although they are positioned in the same place, they are not the same thing. He says one thing and mean two other things and expect you to determine what he really wants. This is why your bucket or relationship list will not work. He cannot read it, understand it and could care less about it. It is your list. The male mind does not process information but subscribe to pleasure. Tell him, I love flowers, and you will probably never get them. Stop him and allow him to look at you and you will get flowers for the rest of your life. He is visual and process what he sees and not what he hears.

You are what he needs, wants and should have but he cannot see you because you are talking. You are hidden. Get up and get into his eyesight. Be seen. Be careful and make sure you are not an eyesore. This is your moment Read Esther, Deborah, Jezebel, Queen of Sheba, Ruth, and Mary Magdalene. They were able to move and shake in the moment. Even the Biblical writer could not leave them out of the scriptures. There is Biblical evidence that man is visual and even the blind man wanted to see. Naomi told Ruth get in Boaz eyesight. She knew he had other maidens, and servants that were at his beck and call. She still encouraged Ruth to get in the midst; Mordechai encouraged Esther to dance for the king; Deborah went to battle even though it was unpopular and unladylike: Jezebel took charge and even though it was considered as evil she was in charge; and the Queen of Sheba taught Solomon how to romance.   There is no need for you to behave unladylike or lose your morals, but you cannot have sat and complain but get up and MOVE. It is about MOVING.

Introduction to Ruth

Ruth is a love story. It is matchmaking at the supreme level. Naomi is the perfect example of a wife, mother, mother-in-law, widow, Christian friend and match-maker. Her life is a splendid example for her daughters-in-law. She was an excellent Christian, devoted wife and wise mother in law. This is why the daughter laws were reluctant to leave her alone. She was their mentor, example and it resulted in great love, respect and attachment. Naomi over the years gained their respect and now they honored her with their desire to be with her. We can also assume that she was a good mother to the sons and a good wife to her husband. If you are seeking the perfect man, maybe you need to look at the perfect example of a mother, wife and friend. Certainly the times are different but the theory is the same. Follow the example set by Naomi and Ruth.

I strongly recommend a reading of the Book of Ruth to see this union between mother and daughter in law. Find a quiet hour or two just to yourself and digest this book of romance and intimacy between these biblical characters. In my opinion Naomi is the ultimate matchmaker. The Book was written during the times of Judges. Samuel, the prophet is the writer. It is a time of great instability and trouble in Israel (Judges 21:25) The Book of Ruth reveals a woman that has lost all of her sons along with her husband but not her faith in God and God's ability to provide. Naomi has nothing left in this world except her daughter in laws and her faith in God. Naomi has no material possessions and no way of obtaining any. She discovers that all of her daughters in laws had an inseparable love for her, but Ruth's love is without limits. Naomi instructs her daughter in laws according to the scripture and law of the land to seek new relationships and husbands. She does not fail in her duty to teach them to be good women, marry, and care for their husband and family. Instructions on relationships began at home. There were not many men available for these women to marry in that area. They were not of the same faith as Naomi, so she admonishes them to return to their own land and find husbands to provide for them. With a great deal of reluctance and sorrow, all of them returned except Ruth. Ruth could not leave her mother in law and Naomi did not have the heart to refuse her companion ship. Ruth is a special daughter in law to Naomi. Ruth found favor in the eyes of Naomi. She becomes the responsibility of Naomi. Naomi accepts the responsibility of Ruth as a special daughter in law. Naomi is duty-bound to see her cared for and hopefully married. Naomi is aware that marriage is the will of God and the law of the land. The daughter-in-law is young, naive, fearful and timid. Naomi is mature, strong, knowledgeable and encouraging.

Naomi is without material substance and the necessities of life. She has no others sons to wed or care for Ruth, who is unwilling to separate from Naomi. She must find a way to honorably care for herself and her daughter in law plus provide some future for Ruth. This is an awesome responsibility, but she relies on God for help. Naomi, who is the principal character in this book serves as a silent matchmaker of her daughter-in-law Ruth and Boaz. The character to watch is not Ruth but Naomi. It is this godly woman who watches for her daughter in law and skillfully put the couple Ruth and Boaz together. Naomi uses her knowledge of customs and traditions as well as her historical knowledge of Boaz to put the two together in a marital relationship. Ruth is in the middle and at times unaware of what was happening. Ruth was obedient. She blindly followed her mother in law instruction. What faith placed in another person. God too requires our obedience.

There are several things that took place in the Book of Ruth:

1. There was a great display of Ruth incredible faith in and love for Naomi.

2. Naomi knowledge of God, tradition, and an unfailing eye for a good and godly man.

3. Both women had unfailing faith and trust in God.

4. Ruth was obedient to the guidance of her mother-in-law.

The Book of Ruth is a beautiful romantic drama in which we see God's love for and care of the homeless, downtrodden and especially the family. It shows that there can be love for a godly mother in law by the daughter in law. It dis-spell the theory of busy body mother in law. This book teaches us the need to know one's self as well as traditions and family history. This book also teaches us the necessity of knowing oneself and one's culture tradition and laws of God and man. There are negotiating skills, promises, and naughtiness. Just as Naomi skillfully put Ruth and Boaz together so can God help each of you find that special mate. You must do something first. Evaluate yourself; know yourself; listen to yourself; and allow God to direct yourself. All that glitter is not gold, but true gold does glitter. Don't throw away the package without looking inside. Don't be fooled by fancy wrappings. God has a way of answering our prayers that will fool even the elect of God. God is a provider of our spiritual, financial and worldly needs. God is too wise to allow a shortage of mates. We will study the Book of Ruth in its entirety verse by verse. The reader should look for the will of and the provisions provided by God for healthy, godly relationships.

BOOK OF RUTH

The first chapter of this book gives us the names of its central characters and their roles. Naomi is now without a husband, sons or any material possessions. This godly woman has lost through death both her husband and her sons. She is alone with three young daughters-in-law to care for. She is ultimately responsible for her daughter-in-law but Naomi is without material resources. The daughter in laws cling to Naomi seeking advice because she was known as a godly woman and these daughter in laws depended on her for instructions and guidance. She advises them to return to their homeland and find husbands and start new families. Apparently these young women were still capable of bearing children. Naomi's advice was accepted by the women, except Ruth. Although all three were concerned about the welfare of the mother in law, Ruth loved her mother in law and would not leave her. She is willing to give up her heritage and youth to follow Naomi and learn the customs of Naomi's people. Naomi return to her homeland destitute and without resources. She must rely on the generosity of her family. Naomi is a wise and compassionate woman, yet aware of her responsibilities as a widow and mother-in-law. She knows Ruth does not know the ways of her people. Ruth is a young, energetic woman full of youth and beauty. She is not aware of what lies ahead. She is willingly to learn and be taught. Naomi in her wisdom knows the way and must guide Ruth. Naomi is aware of the foolishness of youth as well as the uncertainness of old age. She must move quickly and make provisions for herself as well as Ruth.

Naomi needs a husband for Ruth. She understands the value of a good man, but a husband is the last concern of Ruth. She is unable to see the future. Naomi seeks the union of Ruth and Boaz. She is skillful, cunning and almost deceptive in her method and manner to attach Ruth and Boaz. Naomi is aware of Boaz's history as a decent and honest man. He is also a man of substance who can easily take care of both Ruth and Naomi. Naomi using her knowledge of tradition, customs, craftiness, wisdom, trickery and Ruth own naiveness to start a series of events that will lead to the union of Ruth, Boaz and Naomi.

The Book of Ruth teaches us many of the necessary elements in developing a relationship. When seeking a relationship, one must look to the godly wisdom and guidance of those that have maintained a good marriage and raised families. This person should ordinarily be your mother, but not necessarily. You should pray and ask them to pray with you. You must be willing to follow advice. You must remember that positive relationship development is only for the serious at heart. If you are looking for a sex partner, or a man that meet pre-set standards, this will not work. Take a Bible and read along with us in the Book of Ruth as this love story unfolds.

The name Ruth means "friendship". The Moabite woman is the name of the book and its central character. She is the great grandmother of King David and an ancestress in the line of Jesus. She lived in the time of Eli. The book is written in a poetic form and takes place in scenes, as a play would unfold. These scenes give the reader the conversation as well as the customs of the people. Ruth is an example of life among the common ordinary people. The value of love, marriage, family and customs are seen in the book and it teaches us that God will provide and bless the children of God. This book opens on a sad note of death, a famine in the land, disobedience of a daughter in law and ends with a marriage and rejoicing.

Ruth represents the qualities of a Christian woman. Her spirit and countenance are pleasant. She shows humility, respect for self and others, love of family, kindness, and sincerity toward God. Boaz represents the qualities of a Christian man in his religious demeanor, love of God. Respect for law and family tradition, speech, courtesy in greeting people, promptness in taking care of the poor, championing the cause of the needy, dependability, and refusal of taking advantage of the trust of others.

Naomi represents motherhood, widowhood, goodness, unselfishness and skillfulness. She is wise with God as her guide. Naomi knows what has to happen and request God to do it through her. She is a perfect example of one who uses their own loss to help others. Naomi sees the clouds before the storm and makes preparation, not just for self but others.

CHAPTER ONE

This Book opens on a note of sadness and death. These women have lost all including their husbands. Naomi could have bath in self-pity or been rude to her daughter-in-law but this was not the type of woman she was. She could have made them slaves, held them responsible for her care or blamed them for the death of her sons. Naomi had no visible means of support and care for neither herself nor her daughter-in-law. Her faith in God becomes very important. What would she do? Did her faith specifically address the issues facing Naomi? Would God direct her? It is evident that in the face of discouragement Naomi was an encourager. She was a strong woman who knew both man and God. This was a time of adversity and scarcity. It was also a time to keep a cool head, give firm, clear advice and seek the best possible solution for herself and the daughter-in-law. Naomi must become a leader for the daughter-in-law, advise them well and according to the scripture. How many times in your life have you been the focal point of decisions that affect others? Do we inquire of God? Will God respond in time? The present as well as the future depends on Naomi exhibiting the right attitude and giving the daughter-in-law sound and solid advice. She cannot be overly concerned with her own grief and suffering. The requirement of parenthood is never easy nor are the decisions parents must make. A right relationship with God is important in decision-making. Setting a good example make it easy for children to follow the advice and directions of parents. The scripture has specifically commanded the older women to teach and train the younger. When seeking companionship, look for advice from those who by example have maintained a good and prosperous relationship.

Advice is so easy to give, but the lifestyle a person lives is more credible. Naomi not only correctly advised the young women, but secured their trust and admiration. She was concerned about their well-being and following correct principles.

V-1- When Judges ruled means the story took place during the time of the Book of Judges. Famine in the land means, "a depression, a recession, starvation and lack of physical substance "for God 's people. Bethlehem-Judah was a town where David lived and Jesus would later be born. Moab was the son of Lot from an incestuous relationship. (Gen. 19:36) The Moabites and the Israelites throughout history were enemies. They held Israel in servitude for eighteen years. This was a difficult time for God's people. This verse describes a dismal environmental conditions of poverty, depression and captivity. These conditions could have an impact on any decisions made.

V-2-Elimelech means, "My God, my king". Naomi means, "My pleasant one". Marlon means, "Puny or sick". Chilin means, "Pinning". Ephrata was the ancient name of Bethlehem, which means," house of bread". Ruth means "beauty" Names often reflected character, physical condition or desire of the parent for the child. Naming children was done with great consideration.

V-3-5- Naomi husbands is dead. He had prior to this death, left his tribe to live among the enemies, the Moabites. Naomi being faithful followed her husband. The sons of Naomi inter-married with the women of Moab. The Israelites were forbidden to marry Canaanites. (Dt. 7:3 23:3) Naomi and her husband were Israelites who lived among the Moabites. Oprah means, "stiff-necked" and Ruth means," friendship and beauty. Naomi lost in death, her husband and two sons over a ten-year period. This family tragedy, the famine in the land and now the responsibility of caring and advising three young daughter-in-law required a strong godly and unselfish spirit. (Lev 26: Dt. 28)

V-6-9-Naomi heard that God had blessed Israel and wanted to return home. Even in the famine God is still God and He will provide. Her daughter in laws wanted to go also, but she attempted to send them home with her blessings of rest and hope of a second marriage for them. These young ladies were still young enough for marriage and maintaining a family. Naomi was aware of the difference in customs of her people and the ways of the Moabites. She felt the Daughter-in-laws would be better accepted living among their own people. They were still child-bearing age and could receive a husband. It was not too late for them to start new families. She properly instructs and encourages then to return home and do the right thing. This must have been heart-breaking for Naomi to now separate from the daughter-in-law, but she was determined to instruct the daughter-in-law properly. Instructions in relationships must be received from an unselfish source.

V-10-13-She insisted that they return home and find new husbands. She could not bear anymore sons for them to marry. The Israelite law required a man to marry his brother's wife and raise a family in memory of his brother's name. (Deut. 25:5 Matt. 22:23-28) Naomi viewed her tragedy as an act of God's judgment against her. She was not bitter, but accepting of her plight. She must remain in good spirit to encourage her daughter-in-law. Although Naomi herself was going through a difficult and discouraging time, she held her emotions and encouraged her daughter-in-law. Many times we must let go of our problems, emotions and feelings to answer and encourage those who seek advice or those who do not know the way. She advises her daughter-in-law according to the law and what was good for them. Naomi did not take into consideration her own loneliness, and lack of substance.

V-14-18-The three women cried because of their closeness and love for one another. Oprah left, but Ruth stayed. Entreat me not to leave thee means," do not insist that I return". Ruth proclaimed her desire to become a follower of the Lord and customs of the people of Israel. This great testimony of Ruth and her personal commitment would lead to great blessings. Ruth knew that staying with Naomi required learning the customs of the people and obedience to her mother-in-law. Success and status in life is often determined by our obedience to God, laws and people.

V-19-20-Elimelech, Naomi's husband family was well known. Naomi and Ruth were welcomed. She asked that she not be called Naomi, but Mara, which means," bitter" for she was full of sorrow and grief. The loss of her husband and sons in death and the lack of substance to provide for herself were humiliating. This was a humbling experience for Naomi. Many times we find strength with God in the midst of humbling experiences. Ruth grew strong as she witnesses the strength, and faith of Naomi.

V-21-22-Naomi accused God of making her life hard and unbearable. She blames God for her sorrows and failures. Afflicted here does not mean physical sickness or disease but she was poverty-stricken. Who can we blame when life turns into a tragedy or we are faced with a dark moment? Naomi knew God and did not honestly that God had forgotten her. She speaks in a moment of stress, hopelessness and fear. In the beginning of the harvest was about April of the year. "Mara means "bitter" full of "sorrow".

Chapter Two

This chapter opens with more tragedy. It shows the compassion, wisdom, love and strength of a God-fearing mother in law. Naomi lived a life before her daughter in laws that gained their respect and loyalty. Though in great spiritual pain, she desired and did what was best for the women. They were obedient, sincere, and followers of her advice. When seeking advice on relationships we must look to those who have our best interest at heart. They themselves must be maintainers of good relationships and have a positive attitude about life and be encourager. Chapter one gives us an insight into the character of God in the person of Naomi and the followers of God in the person of the daughter in laws. Look for what you want in a relationship in someone who is or have already maintained a relationship.

Chapter two opens with the character Boaz. Women must have a target. Opening yourself up to nothing will result in achieving and achieving nothing. Set a standard for yourself coupled with what can be bendable, breakable and negotiated. Know what you want. Ruth recognize Boaz and set out to find favor in his eyes. Women should sit down with someone who know how to and be told what it takes to raise a family. What qualities do I want in my mate? How do I get into his eyesight? The woman is never to pursue the man but there is nothing wrong with putting yourself in his eyesight. The scripture tells us that "he who finds a wife finds a good thing and has favor with God."

V-1-Boaz means "friend". He was the wealthiest man in town and related to Naomi. Naomi knew the plan for kinsman redemption. Boaz was the target. He exhibited all the qualities necessary for a perfect mate to Ruth and son-in-law for Naomi. Target and tag the man. Boaz was Naomi's choice for Ruth.

V-2-Gleaning was an activity of the poor people who followed reapers and picked up the scraps. It was a right guaranteed to the poor people (Lev.19: 9), and to widows (Deut.24: 19). Finding grace from a landlord means getting permission to glean in his fields. Ruth was in the right place at the right time for a man to show her favor. She presented and placed herself in a position to be shown favor. Ruth went with the expectation of receiving grace from a man and the result of that grace was to be a gleaner in his fields. We should always dress, walk, talk and present ourselves to receive favor. There is nothing to be ashamed of when we are at our best. Your attitude helps your altitude. Your dress exhibits you desire for success. Your talk must match your walk. There is nothing wrong with favor and getting into the eyesight of what you desire. Eye appeal is first, before brain and substance.

V-3-The custom of Israel was the corners of the field were to be left to the poor. (Lev.19: 9-10) Deut. 24:1, 9 Job 24:10) Hap means good luck or happy. Was it luck or divine intervention or was it Naomi's plan? Naomi was a woman of prayer and planning. You must plan to win. Put God first in the plan and pray for divine guidance and intervention.

V-4-7- Ruth by the divine providence of God was led to Boaz field. The direction of our lives are not by accident, but according to the will of God. Boaz came to the field and greeted his workers with a blessing and they in turn pronounced a blessing on him. He noticed Ruth right away and asks of her family heritage. The servant explained that she was Naomi's daughter in law, but a very good worker. Ruth was in the right place at the right time. She was not lazy, but work so hard that the men compliment her work to Boaz. It is not good to have a good plan and no one to work it. You must plan but work the plan. God need something and someone to work with. Ruth made a name for herself as a good worker. What do another think about you? It is also good to know some family history. Boaz inquired and received a character reference.

V-8-10-Recognizing she was Naomi's daughter in law, Boaz realized that she was no ordinary gleaner but a family member. He personally speaks to Ruth and allowed her to follow his maidens. Boaz did not take to chance that she might go to another field, so he immediately began making provisions for her. Maidens were women whose provision Boaz was responsible for providing. He instructed the young men not to touch Ruth. Could this be a sign of interest? He took pity on her or was it interest in her?   Bowing was to show respect and humility. Ruth bows and asks Boaz why he has shown her such grace. Such humility!!   He states that," he is impressed with her love loyalty and respect shown Naomi." Is he sending Naomi a message of interest in Ruth? Is this a quiet interest?   How we treat our parents and those who care for us do not go un-noticed by man or God. Giving of respect allows us to receive respect. It is not disrespecting yourself by showing you are thankful, humble or submissive.

V-11-14-Boaz made it clear, he was aware of her conversion to Christianity and of her decision to leave her people land and her God to help Naomi. Boaz has a great deal of information. Boaz will show the same kindness to Ruth, she showed to her mother in law. "Be not deceived for God is not mocked, whatsoever a man sowed that shall he reap." Is Ruth reaping the kindness shown by her? This is the same love that God wants us to show toward each other. The poor and needy are God's people as well as the rich and powerful. Boaz had a Christ like spirit and Ruth exhibits the Spirit of church. She who had nothing and was nothing, because of a changed attitude will have it all. Attitude-Attitude-Attitude. Boaz begins to fall in love with the attitude of Ruth. He invites her to come and eat with him. Where are all the other maidens? Ruth limited the choices. Eye appeal gets attention, but attitude maintains it.

V-15-16-Boaz blessed Ruth. Gleaning among the sheerer was a rare opportunity. Boaz also left instructions that she was not to be rebuked or touched and the sharers were to drop handfuls of grain purposefully for her to pick up. A childless widowed, a foreign girl, because of her love and devotion and kindness to Naomi will meet a man who would change her life. Ruth immediately became the object of Boaz attention. It was Ruth attitude, mannerism, kindness and ladylike manners that attracted Boaz. It was also God's divine plan. Are you in God's divine plan? Do you know God's plan for your life? Do you have a godly mother or mother in law whose example you can follow or do you think you can do it on your own?

V-17-18-An ephod was one bushel and three pints. It weighed about sixty pounds. Ruth brought the left over from her lunch with Boaz to her mother in law. What a wonderful thought and it impressed Boaz. Naomi was pleased that Ruth met Boaz. He was kin.

V-19-23-Ruth outlined the day's activities to Naomi. Naomi knew the customs and now sets in motion the union of Ruth and Boaz. Naomi knew that Boaz could redeem them both. This was a just man who abided by the law. He could marry Ruth and produce children and preserve the seed of Naomi's husband and sons. She also knew that he was in the line to be the next kinsman. The responsibility of the kinsman was to ensure that the property remain in the family and therefore the obligation rested upon him to marry the widow of a fellow family member who had died childless. Naomi encouraged Ruth to go to the fields and fast with the maidens of Boaz.

CHAPTER THREE

God notice people of good character. (Isa.66:2 1Sam. 16:7) God is not impressed with wealth, power or fame. "It is he who gives us power to get wealth." Be patient and committed to God and God will bless you. (Roman 6:7 Gal. 6:9) In this chapter there is a looks at the integrity of a man, obedience of a daughter and the following of the instructions of God. Boaz did not take advantage of Ruth status and position but empowered her, Naomi gave instruction to Ruth including how to dress. What detail, obedience and faith in another person. What reliance on customs, traditions and God?

V-1-2- The events of the third chapter involves a levirate marital principle of the Hebrews. (Deut. 25:5-6) I was the custom when a man could become obligated to marry his brother's wife or the redemption of property of a deceased relative to provide an heir. Naomi has a claim on Boaz, but allows Ruth to replace her. This again is the showing of true love between the two women. Naomi's plan was to use the right of kinsman redemption to bring Ruth and Boaz together. This right went to the next of kin of a deceased man who had died without any sons or property. Everything was sold in poverty. The families in Israel received their land by lots and these lots were permanent inheritance. Whenever one sold his lot because of poverty, it was the duty of the nearest of kin to buy it back. If not redeemed it would return to the family in the year of jubilee. Naomi's husband had a portion of land, which Naomi had sold in poverty. Boaz was a potential redeemer. According to the law whosoever redeemed the land must also take the wife of the dead brother and rise up the seed in Israel to keep the name alive. The term rest means, "Marriage". Winnowing was done at night because of the coolness and the breeze. It was a method of separating the wheat from the chaff by throwing it into the air and the wheat falling to the ground and the wind taking the chaff away. It is customary for the landowner to oversee this and it was exhausting so Boaz would be tired. Naomi sets the master plan in motion. She knows the custom of the land and the character of the man.

V-3-7-Naomi advises Ruth to clean and beautify herself. Women should be attractive and clean both in personal hygiene and dress. She was not to reveal herself to Boaz, but to mark his sleeping place. Find out where he was sleeping. The term uncovers his feet refers to a morally acceptable custom in which the woman would pull back the edge of a man's robe and lay until noticed. This was a method of proposing and asking to be taken into his house as his wife. Deut. 22:30 Ezek. 16:8. It was the custom in these times that when a woman was to bed with her lawful husband, she would through modesty and subjection to him by going to the foot of the bed and raising the covers and crawling up to the place next to him. These are customs Ruth would not know without the instructions of a knowledgeable mother-in-law. Who said a woman should not ask a man to marry or suggest marriage? Get in his eyesight and wait--don't move!!

"Lack of this knowledge" meant Ruth must have detailed instructions and she must follow them without reservations. What a matchmaker Naomi is! Naomi informs Ruth that Boaz will tell her what to do next and to follow his instructions. Follow the godly man's instructions.

V-8- Boaz woke up afraid. He asks who she was and asks why she was there. It was dark and he did not recognize her immediately.

V-9- Ruth revealed who she was and proposed. "Spread thy skirt" over thy handmaiden was a symbol of taking her under your protection and into your home. When marriage was solemnized among the Jews the man threw his robe over his wife and covered her head.

31

V-10- The tables turned on Boaz. He recognized that he had not fulfilled his duty to redeem Ruth. Boaz was considerably older that Ruth, but age is not an issue. There are things more important than age like happiness, love, peace, joy and provision. He apologized for not redeeming her sooner and doing his kinsman duty. Deut. 25:5-10. Naomi knew he would do the proper thing and redeem Ruth. Boaz was not upset at her. Modesty just went out of the window. A woman must know when to exert herself.

V-11-12-Ruth was within her legal right to request redemption and Boaz quickly and without reservation accepted the right to redeem Ruth. One or the main reason is that she was a virtuous woman and everyone knew it. Who can find a virtuous woman for her price is far above rubies and she made the first move. A man that findeth a wife findeth a good thing but the woman that find a good husband finds a good thing and both enjoys favor with God. It is alright to make the first move as a woman but remain a woman. A godly man will keep your indiscretions a secret Boaz also informs Ruth that there is another kinsman closer than he, so keep her mouth shut.

V-13-15-Boaz told Ruth that if the kinsman didn't do his part then he would redeem her. Boaz told her to lie there until morning. She left before anyone awoke with instructions not to tell anyone of her whereabouts. He sent her away with a veil of barley. A gift and an assurance. What a bad girl Ruth was to stay all night with a man, sleep in his bed and propose marriage to him. She creeps out in the morning with instruction to be quiet.

V-16-18- Ruth returned home with great excitement and told her mother in law all that had happened. How can you confide in mother that you have done such a devious thing? It was the natural order of the day. WAKE UP WOMEN! Boaz did not go hunting, Ruth did. Naomi told her to relax and be calm for Boaz would do as he had said. Naomi was wise.

CHAPTER FOUR

This chapter shows the cleverness, of Boaz. He was a godly man of courage, wisdom and even-handedness. The task of redemption for Ruth required skillful insight. Boaz also wanted the good wishes of all those who would witness the subsequent marriage. Boaz travels to the gate to meet with the elders. It is apparent that Boaz is a man of authority because he calls all the ten Elders together with little notice. He wants the redemption to be public and above board. This is another example of the honesty and integrity of a fair and honorable man. A woman should not only desire but look for these qualities in a marital partner. Being fair and honorable in dealings with the world is a foretaste of the marital union. There were others ahead of Boaz to redeem Ruth. Boaz is aware of their rights of redemption as well as what he has to do to redeem Ruth. The near kinsman is approached first and he refused to redeem Ruth citing his recent marriage and birth of child.

There are seven steps in kinsman redemption:

1. There must be ten witnesses to confirm every transaction between all parties involved as possible redeemers:

2. Agreement on which man shall be redeemer;

3. Taking off the shoe of the one who gives up his right of redemption to another as a witness that he gives up the right;

4. Redemption of the inheritance;

5. Marriage between the redeemer and the wife of the dead one to be raise up seed to continue his name;

6. Confession of witnesses to the transaction;

7. Blessing the married person;

V-1-2-Boaz went to the gate where business was transacted and he waited for the kinsman who has first right to Naomi and Ruth. Boaz apparently had some authority and respect with these Elders. They sat and immediately started to transact business according to the wishes of Boaz. If Boaz could execute such authority in business matters, he would likewise be successful in the handling of family matters

V-3-6- He first tells the kinsman of Naomi and Ruth plight and asked the near kinsman of his right to redeem them. The kinsman agrees to do so. He agreed to redeem the land until it was found the bargain-included marriage to Ruth. The near kinsman was not interested in Ruth. Boaz had no interest in the land but in Ruth. Boaz held his peace to further his plan to redeem Ruth. The kinsman wanted the land because it would make him richer, but not the women. Ruth was poor, from a strange land and a beggar. It was a disgrace to his family and lifestyle to take Ruth and Naomi. He gave up the right to redeem and Boaz right to redeem vested.

V-7-8- It was the custom in Israel at that time when a man gave up a piece of property he took off his shoe in the gate before the elders. This was a sign of the transfer of any rights to property. Boaz has the right to redeem the property with Naomi and Ruth. The passing of the shoe made it a legal transaction. It was also a sign of fair and open dealing among the men. Boaz did not undermine the kinsman but honestly and honorable did the transaction.

V-9-10- Boaz openly declared ownership of all that was Elimelech's, Mahlon and Chilton including Naomi and Ruth. Boaz interest was not in the land as much as in Ruth, a virtuous and prudent woman. She was of great value and a special gift from God. Boaz would also provide comfort for his mother in law Naomi. He was not ashamed of her poverty, heritage and social status in life. Ruth was accepted as already in the house of Boaz. The Elders prayed for the marriage; it's prosperity, success, peace and unity. There was prayer for the fruitfulness of the marriage. The public declaration of marriage to Ruth showed the honor and respect for Ruth.

V-11-12- Many people besides the ten elders witnessed the transaction. The Lord was called upon to bless the marriage with children and fame. Marriage is maintained through trust and prayer. The welfare and prosperity of the marriage is based in large part on well-wishers. The phrase, "Rachel and Leah rather than Sarah and Rebekah" means Sarah and Rebekah each had one child but caused much discord and separation. Rachel and Leah ad many children and built up the house of Israel. "house of Pharez" speak to enlarging the territory and substance of Boaz and Ruth.

V-13-This was the beginning of the family of Boaz. They conceived a son. Ruth was in charge of those whom she once gleaned with in the fields. Psalm 113:7-9 127:3 Isa. 54:1

V-14- This was a joyful ending in the life of Naomi who thought that God had cursed her to a life of poverty and hopelessness. The women who once scorned her now praise her and wished her well.

V-15-Boaz did restore life to Naomi and Ruth and he became famous in Israel. Ruth was better than seven sons to Naomi. She became nurse to the baby. The neighbor named the baby Obed meaning, "serving" which suggest a life of service and devotion. Obed is the father of Jesse who is the father of David.

V-18-22-Generations of Pharez.

Conclusion

The Book of Ruth starts with a bitter woman who had lost everything but her faith in God. Devolping, maintaining and nurturing good relationships depends on our relationships with God. In this book, God provided an angel that saw beyond her loss and imperfection to become attached and responsible. God saw a future of happiness and glory. Isn't it a wonderful experience to see the graciousness of God amid our depression, angry and sorrow for ourselves. God has already worked the situation out; we just need to play it out in our lives. It is in God's plan that we succeed and have positive relationships. The Book of Ruth reveals the need for women of today to honor and respect parents and elders. The Book of Ruth is about God' use of simple ordinary people with morals, principles and a divine purpose. The bonds of love, the wisdom of the aged and the grace of God are expressed in the book of Ruth. God's grace and mercy includes all people regardless of status and position in life. It is he who has developed a divine plan for your life and relationship. There is a plan for you. God is the director of this story and your life story (plan). He takes tragedy, sorrows and troubles through a series of events in life to transform them into peace, joy, love and a complete marital relationship. Steadfast love, loyalty, salvation and kindness are all part of God's plan. The value of a human being is important to God. The happiness and success of the individual is important to God. He wants to bless you in your relationships. The Book of Ruth also teaches us the necessity of those parents living a godly life. It provides balance and hope for the children.

Marriage and relationship is not for everybody. Comparison of relationships can do a dis-service to your own relationship. All relationships are unique and special. Learn to trust your partner as you trust God. Grow in grace and truth with God.

There are many factors to consider when looking for a life partner and many of those qualities are within you rather than without. Relationship requires patience, humility, submission and of course the right partner's. Each partner must nurture each other but the power is in a relationship with God. The materialistic things are also necessary in a relationship, but only to the extent they provide physical substance. These things last a season but love, joy and peace are forever. Money is spent; houses decay; clothing become worn; health decline; and physical strength become physical weakness but true love prevails.

Perfection is not necessary in success relationship, but love and mutual respect should be. There are were women in the genealogy of Jesus. (Matt. 2:1-7) Tamar (Genesis 38:3): Rehab (Joshua 2:5); Ruth: wife of Uriah and Mary his mother. The closest one to flawless character was Mary, Jesus mother. God count both our failures and successes. The failure to work on the successes to grow with. A relationship should be forever growing, never stagnated and definitely changing.

Enter the relationship as you enter God's presence with boldness. Take a chance, reach out, look out and glow, grow and make a commitment to make it work. And if it doesn't, start all over again. Without boldness there are no blessing. Without divine interventions what are the chances that Ruth and Boaz would meet each other? The divine hand of God, who loves a contrite spirit (Isaiah 66:2) puts Ruth, a descendant of Lot, Gentile and Boaz the son of Rahab, the harlot together from which shall be born Jesse, King David and the messiah Jesus.

Wow, what a relationship. God love for all people and can turn your bitterness into a wonderful experience.

The Book of Ruth is a remarkable example of faith, patience, virtue and courage. Two women of opposite faith, yet binding blind love obedience and respect for each other brought about a divine plan of God.

Jesus became our kinsman John 1:14 Eph. 1:7 and it is he that has come to redeem us.

Stop looking for love and accept it; stop complaining and start reigning.

Ernest L. Sanders is a Presiding Bishop in the Episcopal Church of Jesus. He lives in Birmingham, Alabama. He received his Bachelor of Science from Troy State University, M.S, of Theology from Sunbelt Christian College M.S.Walden University and J.D from Miles School of Law. He has done additional studies at the university of Georgia, Augusta College, and Hood theological Seminary.

Bishop Sanders grew up in Montgomery, Alabama. He pastored in the AME Zion Church and the Episcopal Church of Jesus. He was elevated to the status of Presiding Bishop August 2010. He has published many articles and written extensively on the Bible and issues relating to the church.

Other Books by this Authors

Joshua Principle
Study to Show Thyself Approved
Power Failure in the Church

These Books may be ordered through:

Episcopal Publications

Post Office Box 28485

Midfield, Alabama 35160

May be ordered through your local bookstore or Amazon.com

www.ingramcontent.com/pod-product-compliance
Lightning Source LLC
Chambersburg PA
CBHW051050030426
42339CB00006B/285